Help That Cat!

by Jessica Quilty

illustrated by Ilene Richa

Scott Foresman
is an imprint of

Glenview, Illinois • Boston, Massachusetts • Mesa, Arizona
Shoreview, Minnesota • Upper Saddle River, New Jersey

Every effort has been made to secure permission and provide appropriate credit for photographic material. The publisher deeply regrets any omission and pledges to correct errors called to its attention in subsequent editions.

Unless otherwise acknowledged, all photographs are the property of Pearson.

Photo locations denoted as follows: Top (T), Center (C), Bottom (B), Left (L), Right (R), Background (Bkgd)

Illustrations by Ilene Richards

Photograph 12 Getty Images

ISBN 13: 978-0-328-39289-6
ISBN 10: 0-328-39289-8

1 2 3 4 5 6 7 8 9 10 V010 17 16 15 14 13 12 11 10 09 08

"Look at that cat!" I said.

I watched as a little yellow cat ran by as fast as it could go. Then I saw a big dog running after the cat. I saw Mr. Green run by too.

Jen, Jon, Kix, and I all ran after Mr. Green, the dog, and the cat. We stopped at the park.

"Where did it go?" said Kix.

We looked here. We looked there. But we did not see the little yellow cat.

"Look! Look up in the tree. There is my cat!" Mr. Green said.

At the bottom of the big tree sat the big dog. He looked up at the cat too.

"Let me get your cat," I said to Mr. Green.

The tree was too big. I was too little. I could not climb it.

I ran to find help.

"Can you help?" I asked a police officer in a blue hat. "Mr. Green's little cat is up in a big tree!"

Officer Kim smiled. "I can be of service!" she said. "I can help Mr. Green and his cat."

She took out her police radio. "Get the fire department! Mr. Green has a little cat up in a big tree!"

We all looked up. There was the little yellow cat, still in the big tree.

We looked down. There was the dog, still by the tree. We looked back up.

"Look at that cat!" said Officer Kim.

Then the big firefighter came.

"Look at that cat!" he said. "I can get that cat down in no time flat. I have the tools for this job!"

"Excuse me, please," he said to the dog and climbed up a ladder.

"Oh, look!" said Officer Kim.

"Be careful!" said Mr. Green.

The firefighter reached for the cat when it came close.

"Look at that cat!" I said.

We all walked to the vet. We wanted to make sure the cat was well. The dog followed close behind.

"Let me take a look," said the vet. She looked at the head, the tail, and all four paws.

"This is the healthiest cat I have seen in my whole career as a vet!" she said.

Suddenly the big dog barked. The cat began to run.

"Oh no!" we all said.

But the little yellow cat did not go far. She went over to the big dog. The cat licked the dog right on the nose!

And everybody said, "Look at that cat!"

Jobs That Help

Some people choose jobs that let them help out in their communities. We rely on firefighters, police officers, and doctors to help us stay safe. Other jobs help people too. Think about all of the people you know who do helping jobs. How many helping jobs do you know about?